Happiness 365:
One-a-day Inspirational Quotes for a
Happy YOU

By
Deena B. Chopra and KC Harry
*Book One of the Happiness 365 Inspirational
Series*

HAPPINESS 365: ONE-A-DAY INSPIRATIONAL QUOTES FOR A HAPPY YOU

First edition. August 31, 2014.

Written by Deena B. Chopra and KC Harry.

10 9 8 7 6 5 4 3 2 1

This eBook is dedicated to you and your ongoing happiness.

Happiness 365 Quotes direct to your inbox daily.

And be the first to learn of Happiness 365 updates, giveaways, free days and new books in the series.

Sign up here:
http://www.kcharry.com/happiness-365-updates/
And like us on Facebook to join the conversation!
https://www.facebook.com/pages/Happiness-365/1441747622781692

Foreword

Imagine you can't sleep at night, because you're so excited to start the day. You would celebrate your ability to jump out of bed, set a goal and live into it while also taking the twists and turns of life as they come. The Happiness 365 Inspirational Series is a simple series of eBooks which will give you a quick emotional boost, right when you ask for it. And you will potentially find yourself able to enjoy more, be a joy to your family, and see a tangible change all around you. This book is a gift to you, from us. Enjoy and be happy.

Introduction

We know this to be true: It's a given that life is not about rainbows and sunshine all of the time. There will be days that it is going to be hard to hold your head high and put a smile on your face. However, happiness is a choice; and sometimes, you just occasionally need a boost to remind yourself of that fact.

It is intuitive that people who smile and cut out negativity from their life will live longer, healthier lives. You hear it in TED talks, read it on blogs, and physicians (and psychologists) use it as a mantra. Stress and anger cause health complications that make life harder than it needs to be. It will also leave you with higher medical bills, which will cause more stress if you are struggling financially.

This book is designed to help give you that small happiness boost you may require at any time. It provides a variety of quotes, new and older, to help you put perspective on your mood, regardless of where you are at in your life. It is organized for quotes to be consumed once per day, however we welcome you to peruse through the pages until you find one that resonates with you at that specific moment.

No matter who you are, be it a teenager or in later stages of life, whether you are married or divorced, an entrepreneur or a career professional, or even unemployed, choosing to be happy helps you in all facets of your life. Take it a day at a time, and find the quotes that speak to your needs for the day. Read, reflect and refocus when the stress and trials of the day attempt to derail your mood.

You deserve to be happy so find it in your mind.

PS: This is a simple paperback version of the eBook. It has an additional journaling feature, which that allows you to journal each morning by drawing inspiration from the quote you select for that day. You can also follow along with Deena and KC as they share each day's quote by email and on social media, and turn this journey into an inspirational worldwide community discussion.

Join us! We're on Twitter at:

Deena: https://twitter.com/DeenaBChopra

KC: https://twitter.com/kchrissyharry

One-a-Day Happiness Quotes

Day 1

Thousands of candles can be lit from a single candle, and the life of the candle will not be shortened. Happiness never decreases by being shared.

Buddha

<u>Journaling Exercise: Write your thoughts below.</u>

Day 2

If you want to live a happy life, tie it to a goal, not to people or things.

Albert Einstein

Journaling Exercise: Write your thoughts below.

Day 3

Don't cry because it's over. Smile because it happened.

Dr. Seuss

Journaling Exercise: Write your thoughts below.

Day 4

We tend to forget that happiness doesn't come as a result of getting something we don't have, but rather of recognizing and appreciating what we do have.

Frederick Keonig

<u>Journaling Exercise: Write your thoughts below.</u>

Day 5

All that we are is the result of what we have thought. If you speak or act with an evil thought, pain follows you. If you speak or act with a pure thought, happiness follows you, like a shadow that never leaves you.

Buddha

Journaling Exercise: Write your thoughts below.

Day 6

I, not events, have the power to make me happy or unhappy today. I can choose which it shall be. Yesterday is dead, tomorrow hasn't arrived yet. I have just one day, today, and I'm going to be happy in it.

Groucho Marx

Journaling Exercise: Write your thoughts below.

Day 7

Happiness is the meaning and the purpose of life, the whole aim and end of human existence.

Aristotle

<u>Journaling Exercise: Write your thoughts below.</u>

Day 8

The best years of your life are the ones in which you decide your problems are your own. You do not blame them on your mother, the ecology, or the president. You realize that you control your own destiny.

Albert Ellis

Journaling Exercise: Write your thoughts below.

Day 9

Happiness is an attitude. We either make ourselves miserable, or happy and strong. The amount of work is the same.

Francesca Reigler

Journaling Exercise: Write your thoughts below.

Day 10

Success is not the key to happiness. Happiness is the key to success. If you love what you are doing, you will be successful.

Herman Cain

<u>Journaling Exercise: Write your thoughts below.</u>

Day 11

It is not easy to find happiness in ourselves, and it is not possible to find it elsewhere.

Agnes Repplier

Journaling Exercise: Write your thoughts below.

Day 12

No one is in control of your happiness but you; therefore, you have the power to change anything about yourself or your life that you want to change.

Barbara De Angelis

<u>Journaling Exercise: Write your thoughts below.</u>

Day 13

The (US) Constitution only gives people the right to pursue happiness. You have to catch it yourself.

Benjamin Franklin

Journaling Exercise: Write your thoughts below.

Day 14
Happiness belongs to the self-sufficient

Aristotle

<u>Journaling Exercise: Write your thoughts below.</u>

Day 15

Remember happiness doesn't depend upon who you are or what you have; it depends solely on what you think.

Dale Carnegie

<u>Journaling Exercise: Write your thoughts below.</u>

Day 16

There is only one way to happiness and that is to cease worrying about things which are beyond the power of our will.

Epictetus

Journaling Exercise: Write your thoughts below.

Day 17

A happy person is not a person in a certain set of circumstances, but rather a person with a certain set of attitudes.

Hugh Downs

Journaling Exercise: Write your thoughts below.

Day 18

When one door of happiness closes, another opens; but often we look so long at the closed door that we do not see the one which has been opened for us.

Helen Keller

Journaling Exercise: Write your thoughts below.

Day 19

He (she) who depends on himself (herself) will attain the greatest happiness.

Chinese Proverbs

Journaling Exercise: Write your thoughts below.

Day 20

The moments of happiness we enjoy take us by surprise. It is not that we seize them, but that they seize us.

Ashley Montagu

Journaling Exercise: Write your thoughts below.

Day 21

Happiness is not a goal; it is a by-product.

Eleanor Roosevelt

Journaling Exercise: Write your thoughts below.

Day 22

But what is happiness except the simple harmony between a man and the life he leads?

Albert Camus

Journaling Exercise: Write your thoughts below.

Day 23

Everyone chases after happiness, not noticing that happiness is right at their heels.

Bertolt Brecht

<u>Journaling Exercise: Write your thoughts below.</u>

Day 24

Happiness doesn't depend on any external conditions, it is governed by our mental attitude.

Dale Carnegie

<u>Journaling Exercise: Write your thoughts below.</u>

Day 25

Success, happiness, peace of mind and fulfillment - the most priceless of human treasures - are available to all among us, without exception, who make things happen - who make "good" things happen - in the world around them.

                                                              Joe Klock

Journaling Exercise: Write your thoughts below.

Day 26

Happiness is not something ready-made. It comes from your own actions.

Dalai Lama

Journaling Exercise: Write your thoughts below.

Day 27

If you're respectful by habit, constantly honoring the worthy, four things increase: long life, beauty, happiness, strength.

               Buddha

Journaling Exercise: Write your thoughts below.

Day 28

Happiness is not something you postpone for the future; it is something you design for the present.

Jim Rohn

Journaling Exercise: Write your thoughts below.

Day 29

Pleasure may come from illusion, but happiness can come only of reality.

Chamfort

Journaling Exercise: Write your thoughts below.

Day 30

Happiness is that state of consciousness which proceeds from the achievement of one's values.

Ayn Rand

<u>Journaling Exercise: Write your thoughts below.</u>

Day 31

We have no more right to consume happiness without producing it than to consume wealth without producing it.

George Bernard Shaw

Journaling Exercise: Write your thoughts below.

Day 32

If you want others to be happy, practice compassion. If you want to be happy, practice compassion.

Dalai Lama

Journaling Exercise: Write your thoughts below.

Day 33

As human beings we all want to be happy and free from misery we have learned that the key to happiness is inner peace. The greatest obstacles to inner peace are disturbing emotions such as anger, attachment, fear and suspicion, while love and compassion and a sense of universal responsibility are the sources of peace and happiness.

Dalai Lama

Journaling Exercise: Write your thoughts below.

Day 34

To me, there are three things we all should do every day. We should do this every day of our lives. Number one is laugh. You should laugh every day. Number two is think. You should spend some time in thought. And number three is, you should have your emotions moved to tears, could be happiness or joy. But think about it. If you laugh, you think, and you cry, that's a full day. That's a heck of a day. You do that seven days a week, you're going to have something special.

Jim Valvano

Journaling Exercise: Write your thoughts below.

Day 35

Happiness can exist only in acceptance.

George Orwell

Journaling Exercise: Write your thoughts below.

Day 36

It is not how much we have, but how much we enjoy, that makes happiness.

Charles H. Spurgeon

Journaling Exercise: Write your thoughts below.

Day 37
Happiness is a choice that requires effort at times

Aeschylus

Journaling Exercise: Write your thoughts below.

Day 38

If one advances confidently in the direction of one's dreams, and endeavors to live the life which one has imagined, one will meet with a success unexpected in common hours.

Henry David Thoreau

Journaling Exercise: Write your thoughts below.

Day 39
I believe that the very purpose of our life is to seek happiness. That is clear. Whether one believes in religion or not, whether one believes in this religion or that religion, we all are seeking something better in life. So, I think, the very motion of our life is towards happiness

Dalai Lama

<u>Journaling Exercise: Write your thoughts below.</u>

Day 40

There can be no happiness if the things we believe in are different from the things we do.

Freya Stark

Journaling Exercise: Write your thoughts below.

Day 41

The word 'happiness' would lose its meaning if it were not balanced by sadness.

Carl Gustav Jung

<u>Journaling Exercise: Write your thoughts below.</u>

Day 42

If a man who enjoys a lesser happiness beholds a greater one, let him leave aside the lesser to gain the greater.

Buddha

Journaling Exercise: Write your thoughts below.

Day 43

I believe that the very purpose of life is to be happy. From the very core of our being, we desire contentment. In my own limited experience I have found that the more we care for the happiness of others, the greater is our own sense of well-being. Cultivating a close, warm hearted feeling for others automatically puts the mind at ease. It helps remove whatever fears or insecurities we may have and gives us the strength to cope with any obstacles we encounter. It is the principal source of success in life. Since we are not solely material creatures, it is a mistake to place all our hopes for happiness on external development alone. The key is to develop inner peace.

Dalai Lama

Journaling Exercise: Write your thoughts below.

Day 44

Happiness is an expression of the soul in considered actions.

Aristotle

Journaling Exercise: Write your thoughts below.

Day 45
Nothing prevents happiness like the memory of happiness.

Andre Gide

Journaling Exercise: Write your thoughts below.

Day 46

Happiness is a by-product of an effort to make someone else happy.

Gretta Brooker Palmer

Journaling Exercise: Write your thoughts below.

Day 47

It is not in doing what you like, but in liking what you do that is the secret of happiness.

James Matthew Barrie

Journaling Exercise: Write your thoughts below.

Day 48

The art of living does not consist in preserving and clinging to a particular mood of happiness, but in allowing happiness to change its form without being disappointed by the change, for happiness, like a child, must be allowed to grow up.

Charles Morgan

Journaling Exercise: Write your thoughts below.

Day 49

People take different roads seeking fulfillment and happiness. Just because they're not on your road doesn't mean they've gotten lost.

H. Jackson Brown Jr.

Journaling Exercise: Write your thoughts below.

Day 50

Whoever said you can't buy happiness forgot little puppies.

Gene Hill

Journaling Exercise: Write your thoughts below.

Day 51

If what Proust says is true, that happiness is the absence of fever, then I will never know happiness. For I am possessed by a fever for knowledge, experience, and creation.

Anais Nin

Journaling Exercise: Write your thoughts below.

Day 52

The happiness of too many days is often destroyed by trying to accomplish too much in one day. We would do well to follow a common rule for our daily lives - DO LESS, AND DO IT BETTER.

Dale E. Turner

Journaling Exercise: Write your thoughts below.

Day 53

If our condition were truly happy, we would not seek diversion from it in order to make ourselves happy.

Blaise Pascal

<u>Journaling Exercise: Write your thoughts below.</u>

Day 54

Happiness? That's nothing more than a good health and a poor memory.

Albert Schweitzer

Journaling Exercise: Write your thoughts below.

Day 55

The present is never our goal: the past and present are our means: the future alone is our goal. Thus, we never live but we hope to live; and always hoping to be happy, it is inevitable that we will never be so.

Blaise Pascal

Journaling Exercise: Write your thoughts below.

Day 56

Caring about others, running the risk of feeling, and leaving an impact on people, brings happiness.

Harold Kushner

Journaling Exercise: Write your thoughts below.

Day 57

Your success and happiness lies in you. Resolve to keep happy, and your joy and you shall form an invincible host against difficulties.

Helen Keller

Journaling Exercise: Write your thoughts below.

Day 58

I would maintain that thanks are the highest form of thought, and that gratitude is happiness doubled by wonder.

G. K. Chesterton

Journaling Exercise: Write your thoughts below.

Day 59

They must often change, who would be constant in happiness or wisdom.

Confucius

Journaling Exercise: Write your thoughts below.

Day 60

Happiness is mental harmony; unhappiness is mental 'in-harmony'.

James Allen

<u>Journaling Exercise: Write your thoughts below.</u>

Day 61

Human happiness and human satisfaction must ultimately come from within oneself. It is wrong to expect some final satisfaction to come from money or from a computer.

Dalai Lama

Journaling Exercise: Write your thoughts below.

Day 62

You cannot prevent the birds of sadness from passing over your head, but you can prevent their making a nest in your hair.

Chinese Proverbs

Journaling Exercise: Write your thoughts below.

Day 63

The happiness which brings enduring worth to life is not the superficial happiness that is dependent on circumstances. It is the happiness and contentment that fills the soul even in the midst of the most distressing circumstances and the most bitter environment. It is the kind of happiness that grins when things go wrong and smiles through the tears. The happiness for which our souls ache is one undisturbed by success or failure, one which will root deeply inside us and give inward relaxation, peace, and contentment, no matter what the surface problems may be. That kind of happiness stands in need of no outward stimulus.

Billy Graham

Journaling Exercise: Write your thoughts below.

Day 64

There is nothing to trust seeking happiness from outside, you will only become exhausted with suffering, with is without satisfaction and without end.

Dalai Lama

Journaling Exercise: Write your thoughts below.

Day 65

Virtue and Happiness are Mother and Daughter.

Benjamin Franklin

Journaling Exercise: Write your thoughts below.

Day 66

No one has a right to consume happiness without producing it.

Helen Keller

<u>Journaling Exercise: Write your thoughts below.</u>

Day 67

If you want happiness for a lifetime - help the next generation.

Chinese Proverbs

Journaling Exercise: Write your thoughts below.

Day 68

You must try to generate happiness within yourself. If you aren't happy in one place, chances are you won't be happy anyplace.

Ernie Banks

Journaling Exercise: Write your thoughts below.

Day 69

If one's life is simple, contentment has to come. Simplicity is extremely important for happiness. Having few desires, feeling satisfied with what you have, is very vital: satisfaction with just enough food, clothing, and shelter to protect yourself from the elements. And finally, there is an intense delight in abandoning faulty states of mind and in cultivating helpful ones in meditation.

                                                              Dalai Lama

Journaling Exercise: Write your thoughts below.

Day 70

Men can only be happy when they do not assume that the object of life is happiness

George Orwell

<u>Journaling Exercise: Write your thoughts below.</u>

Day 71

The person who seeks all their applause from outside has their happiness in another's keeping.

Dale Carnegie

Journaling Exercise: Write your thoughts below.

Day 72

May brooks and trees and singing hills join in the chorus too, and every gentle wind that blows send happiness to you.

Irish Blessings

Journaling Exercise: Write your thoughts below.

Day 73

When one door of happiness closes, another opens.

Helen Keller

Journaling Exercise: Write your thoughts below.

Day 74

I don't believe in happy endings, but I do believe in happy travels, because ultimately, you die at a very young age, or you live long enough to watch your friends die. It's a mean thing, life.

George Clooney

Journaling Exercise: Write your thoughts below.

Day 75

Happiness is the absence of the striving for happiness.

Chuang Tzu

Journaling Exercise: Write your thoughts below.

Day 76
There is no happiness like spiritual knowledge.

Chanakya

Journaling Exercise: Write your thoughts below.

Day 77

True happiness comes from the joy of deeds well done, the zest of creating things new.

Antoine de Saint-Exupery

Journaling Exercise: Write your thoughts below.

Day 78

Happy people plan actions, they don't plan results.

Dennis Wholey

Journaling Exercise: Write your thoughts below.

Day 79

Life is like topography, Hobbes. There are summits of happiness and success, flat stretches of boring routine, and valleys of frustration and failure.

Calvin & Hobbes

Journaling Exercise: Write your thoughts below.

Day 80

The habit of being uniformly considerate toward others will bring increased happiness to you.

Grenville Kleiser

Journaling Exercise: Write your thoughts below.

Day 81

The secret of happiness is the determination to be happy always, rather than wait for outer circumstances to make one happy.

J. Donald Walters

<u>Journaling Exercise: Write your thoughts below.</u>

Day 82

Remember that the happiest people are not those getting more, but those giving more.

H. Jackson Brown Jr.

Journaling Exercise: Write your thoughts below.

Day 83

For those who may not find happiness to exercise religious faith, it's okay to remain a radical atheist, it's absolutely an individual right, but the important thing is with a compassionate heart—then no problem.

Dalai Lama

Journaling Exercise: Write your thoughts below.

Day 84

Don't wait around for other people to be happy for you. Any happiness you get you've got to make yourself.

Alice Walker

Journaling Exercise: Write your thoughts below.

Day 85

Be happy. Talk happiness. Happiness calls out responsive gladness in others. There is enough sadness in the world without yours...never doubt the excellence and permanence of what is yet to be.

Helen Keller

Journaling Exercise: Write your thoughts below.

Day 86

If you wish to be happy yourself, you must resign yourself to seeing others also happy.

Bertrand Russell

Journaling Exercise: Write your thoughts below.

Day 87

Happiness and moral duty are inseparably connected.

George Washington

<u>Journaling Exercise: Write your thoughts below.</u>

Day 88

You have it easily in your power to increase the sum total of this world's happiness now. How? By giving a few words of sincere appreciation to someone who is lonely or discouraged. Perhaps you will forget tomorrow the kind words you say today, but the recipient may cherish them over a lifetime.

Dale Carnegie

Journaling Exercise: Write your thoughts below.

Day 89

There is neither this world nor the world beyond nor happiness for the one who doubts.

Bhagavad Gita

Journaling Exercise: Write your thoughts below.

Day 90

Learn to enjoy every minute of your life. Be happy now. Don't wait for something outside of yourself to make you happy in the future. Think how really precious is the time you have to spend, whether it's at work or with your family.

Earl Nightingale

Journaling Exercise: Write your thoughts below.

Day 91

Many persons have a wrong idea of what constitutes true happiness. It is not attained through self-gratification but through fidelity to a worthy purpose.

Helen Keller

<u>Journaling Exercise: Write your thoughts below.</u>

Day 92

It is only a poor sort of happiness that could ever come by caring very much about our own pleasures. We can only have the highest happiness such as goes along with being a great man, by having wide thoughts and much feeling for the rest of the world as well as ourselves.

George Eliot

Journaling Exercise: Write your thoughts below.

Day 93

Happiness is a continuation of happenings which are not resisted.

Deepak Chopra

<u>Journaling Exercise: Write your thoughts below.</u>

Day 94

To be happy, we must not be too concerned with others.

Albert Camus

<u>Journaling Exercise: Write your thoughts below.</u>

Day 95

The happiness of this life depends less on what befalls you than the way in which you take it.

Elbert Hubbard

<u>Journaling Exercise: Write your thoughts below.</u>

Day 96

Being happy is better than being king.

African Proverb

Journaling Exercise: Write your thoughts below.

Day 97

Act as if you were already happy and that will tend to make you happy.

Dale Carnegie

Journaling Exercise: Write your thoughts below.

Day 98

If a man will understand how intimately, yea, how inseparably, self-control and happiness are associated, he has but to look into his own heart, and upon the world around,...Looking upon the lives of men and women, he will perceive how the hasty word, the bitter retort, the act of deception, the blind prejudice and foolish resentment bring wretchedness and even ruin in their train.

James Allen

Journaling Exercise: Write your thoughts below.

Day 99

It is better to be happy for a moment and be burned up with beauty than to live a long time and be bored all the while.

Helen Keller

<u>Journaling Exercise: Write your thoughts below.</u>

Day 100

The trick is in what one emphasizes. We either make ourselves miserable, or we make ourselves happy. The amount of work is the same.

Carlos Castaneda

Journaling Exercise: Write your thoughts below.

Day 101

It's good to be just plain happy, it's a little better to know that you're happy; but to understand that you're happy and to know why and how and still be happy, be happy in the being and the knowing, well that is beyond happiness, that is bliss.

Henry Miller

Journaling Exercise: Write your thoughts below.

Day 102

To enjoy good health, to bring true happiness to one's family, to bring peace to all, one must first discipline and control one's own mind. If a man can control his mind he can find the way to Enlightenment, and all wisdom and virtue will naturally come to him.

Buddha

Journaling Exercise: Write your thoughts below.

Day 103

There is no value in life except what you choose to place upon it and no happiness in any place except what you bring to it yourself.

Henry David Thoreau

<u>Journaling Exercise: Write your thoughts below.</u>

Day 104
Anything you're good at contributes to happiness

Bertrand Russell

<u>Journaling Exercise: Write your thoughts below.</u>

Day 105

True happiness...is not attained through self-gratification, but through fidelity to a worthy purpose.

Helen Keller

<u>Journaling Exercise: Write your thoughts below.</u>

Day 106
The purpose of our lives is to be happy.

Dalai Lama

Journaling Exercise: Write your thoughts below.

Day 107
Happiness is a journey...not a destination.

Ben Sweetland

Journaling Exercise: Write your thoughts below.

Day 108

I can see, and that is why I can be happy, in what you call the dark, but which to me is golden. I can see a God-made world, not a manmade world.

Helen Keller

Journaling Exercise: Write your thoughts below.

Day 109

The secret of happiness is having something meaningful to do, seeking purpose.

John Burroughs

Journaling Exercise: Write your thoughts below.

Day 110

A mother's happiness is like a beacon, lighting up the future but reflected also on the past in the guise of fond memories.

Honore de Balzac

Journaling Exercise: Write your thoughts below.

Day 111

A sure way to lose happiness, I found, is to want it at the expense of everything else

Bette Davis

Journaling Exercise: Write your thoughts below.

Day 112

False happiness renders men stern and proud, and that happiness is never communicated. True happiness renders them kind and sensible, and that happiness is always shared.

Charles de Montesquieu

Journaling Exercise: Write your thoughts below.

Day 113
A great obstacle to happiness is to expect too much happiness.

Fontenelle

Journaling Exercise: Write your thoughts below.

Day 114

All we need to make us really happy is something to be enthusiastic about.

Charles Kingsley

Journaling Exercise: Write your thoughts below.

Day 115
Happiness is a habit - cultivate it.

Elbert Hubbard

Journaling Exercise: Write your thoughts below.

Day 116

Happy is he who still loves something he loved in the nursery: He has not been broken in two by time; he is not two men, but one, and he has saved not only his soul but his life.

G. K. Chesterton

Journaling Exercise: Write your thoughts below.

Day 117

What makes us discontented with our condition is the absurdly exaggerated idea we have of the happiness of others.

French Proverb

<u>Journaling Exercise: Write your thoughts below.</u>

Day 118

Money has never made man happy, nor will it, there is nothing in its nature to produce happiness. The more of it one has the more one wants.

Benjamin Franklin

Journaling Exercise: Write your thoughts below.

Day 119
While we pursue happiness, we flee from contentment.

Hasidic Proverb

Journaling Exercise: Write your thoughts below.

Day 120

Happiness is like a sunbeam, which the least shadow intercepts, while adversity is often as the rain of spring.

Chinese Proverb

Journaling Exercise: Write your thoughts below.

Day 121

Everyone wants happiness; nobody wants to suffer. Many problems around us are a mental projection of certain negative or unpleasant things. If we analyze our own mental attitude, we may find it quite unbearable. Therefore, a well-balanced mind is very useful and we should try and have a stable mental state.

Dalai Lama

Journaling Exercise: Write your thoughts below.

Day 122

Each has his own happiness in his hands, as the artist handles the rude clay he seeks to reshape it into a figure; yet it is the same with this art as with all others: only the capacity for it is innate; the art itself must be learned and painstaking

Johann Wolfgang von Goethe

Journaling Exercise: Write your thoughts below.

Day 123

The happiness of a man in this life does not consist in the absence but in the mastery of his passions.

Alfred Lord Tennyson

<u>Journaling Exercise: Write your thoughts below.</u>

Day 124

Most people ask for happiness on condition. Happiness can only be felt if you don't set any condition.

Arthur Rubinstein

<u>Journaling Exercise: Write your thoughts below.</u>

Day 125

Strength is Happiness. Strength is itself victory. In weakness and cowardice there is no happiness. When you wage a struggle, you might win or you might lose. But regardless of the short-term outcome, the very fact of your continuing to struggle is proof of your victory as a human being.

Daisaku Ikeda

Journaling Exercise: Write your thoughts below.

Day 126

I had looked for happiness in fast living, but it was not there. I tried to find it in money, but it was not there either. But when I placed myself in tune with what I believe to be the fundamental truths of life, when I began to develop my limited ability, to rid my mind of all kinds of tangled thoughts, and fill it with zeal and courage and love, when I gave myself a chance by treating myself decently and sensibly, I began to feel the stimulating, warm glow of happiness.

Edward Young

Journaling Exercise: Write your thoughts below.

Day 127
All happiness depends on a leisurely breakfast.

John Gunther

Journaling Exercise: Write your thoughts below.

Day 128

We all live with the objective of being happy, our lives are all different and yet the same.

Anne Frank

Journaling Exercise: Write your thoughts below.

Day 129

I wish people could achieve what they think would bring them happiness in order for them to realize that that's not really what happiness is.

Alanis Morissette

Journaling Exercise: Write your thoughts below.

Day 130

Be more dedicated to making solid achievements than in running after swift but synthetic happiness.

Abdul Kalam

Journaling Exercise: Write your thoughts below.

Day 131

Happiness is a how; not a what. A talent, not an object.

Hermann Hesse

Journaling Exercise: Write your thoughts below.

Day 132

Success is getting what you want. Happiness is liking what you get.

H. Jackson Brown Jr.

Journaling Exercise: Write your thoughts below.

Day 133

The first recipe for happiness is: Avoid too lengthy meditation on the past.

Andre Maurois

Journaling Exercise: Write your thoughts below.

Day 134

When a small child, I thought that success spelled happiness. I was wrong, happiness is like a butterfly which appears and delights us for one brief moment, but soon flits away.

Anna Pavlova

Journaling Exercise: Write your thoughts below.

Day 135

Knowledge is happiness, because to have knowledge—broad, deep knowledge—is to know true ends from false, and lofty things from low.

Helen Keller

Journaling Exercise: Write your thoughts below.

Day 136

You are forgiven for your happiness and your successes only if you generously consent to share them.

Albert Camus

Journaling Exercise: Write your thoughts below.

Day 137

May flowers always line your path and sunshine light your day. May songbirds serenade you every step along the way. May a rainbow run beside you in a sky that's always blue. And may happiness fill your heart each day your whole life through.

An Irish Blessing

Journaling Exercise: Write your thoughts below.

Day 138

This we can all bear witness to, living as we do plagued by unremitting anxiety. It becomes more and more imperative that the life of the spirit be avowed as the only firm basis upon which to establish happiness and peace.

Dalai Lama

Journaling Exercise: Write your thoughts below.

Day 139

The greatest of follies is to sacrifice health for any other kind of happiness.

Arthur Schopenhauer

<u>Journaling Exercise: Write your thoughts below.</u>

Day 140

Happy is the person who finds wisdom, and he (she) who receives understanding.

Bible

Journaling Exercise: Write your thoughts below.

Day 141

Be unselfish. That is the first and final commandment for those who would be useful and happy in their usefulness. If you think of yourself only, you cannot develop because you are choking the source of development, which is spiritual expansion through thought for others.

Charles W. Eliot

Journaling Exercise: Write your thoughts below.

Day 142

There is the happiness which comes from creative effort. The joy of dreaming, creating, building, whether in painting a picture, writing an epic, singing a song, composing a symphony, devising new invention, creating a vast industry.

Henry Miller

Journaling Exercise: Write your thoughts below.

Day 143

There is no happiness in having or in getting, but only in giving

Henry Drummond

<u>Journaling Exercise: Write your thoughts below.</u>

Day 144

The secret of happiness is this: let your interests be as wide as possible, and let your reactions to the things and persons that interest you be as far as possible friendly rather than hostile.

Bertrand Russell

Journaling Exercise: Write your thoughts below.

Day 145

On the highway of life, we most often recognize happiness out of the rear view mirror.

Frank Tyger

<u>Journaling Exercise: Write your thoughts below.</u>

Day 146

Even a happy life cannot be without a measure of darkness, and the word happy would lose its meaning if it were not balanced by sadness. It is far better take things as they come along with patience and equanimity.

Carl Gustav Jung

Journaling Exercise: Write your thoughts below.

Day 147

One is happy as a result of one's own efforts once one knows the necessary ingredients of happiness' simple tastes: a certain degree of courage, self-denial to a point, love of work, and above all, a clear conscience.

George Sand

Journaling Exercise: Write your thoughts below.

Day 148

Being nice is one of many bridges on the road to Happiness.

Donna A. Favors

Journaling Exercise: Write your thoughts below.

Day 149

Knowledge of what is possible is the beginning of happiness.

George Santayana

Journaling Exercise: Write your thoughts below.

Day 150

The essence of philosophy is that a man should so live that his happiness shall depend as little as possible on external things.

Epictetus

Journaling Exercise: Write your thoughts below.

Day 151

My upbringing made me as I am now. But I can become merry and happy at once. There were many years I was feeling at a loss about my life or how I grew up. I couldn't understand what is right or what is precious. At that time, I was so miserable and self-defeating. I was feeling angry with various things. My anger came up to the surface then. I don't say such tendency has disappeared. Even now there are anger and the dark side in myself. But it's the first time I've been so close to the light.

Johnny Depp

Journaling Exercise: Write your thoughts below.

Day 152

Do you want my one-word secret of happiness? It's growth - mental, financial, you name it.

Harold S. Geneen

Journaling Exercise: Write your thoughts below.

Day 153

Now and then it's good to pause in our pursuit of happiness and just be happy.

Guillaume Apollinaire

Journaling Exercise: Write your thoughts below.

Day 154

Happiness is like those palaces in fairy tales whose gates are guarded by dragons: we must fight in order to conquer it.

Alexandre Dumas Pere

Journaling Exercise: Write your thoughts below.

Day 155

Happiness is a matter of one's most ordinary and everyday mode of consciousness being busy and lively and unconcerned with self.

Iris Murdoch

Journaling Exercise: Write your thoughts below.

Day 156

Happiness is not an ideal of reason but of imagination.

Immanuel Kant

Journaling Exercise: Write your thoughts below.

Day 157

Happiness grows at our own firesides, and is not to be picked in a stranger's gardens.

Douglas William Jerrold

Journaling Exercise: Write your thoughts below.

Day 158
For each petal on the shamrock this brings a wish your way.
Good health, good luck, and happiness for today and every day.

An Irish Blessing

Journaling Exercise: Write your thoughts below.

Day 159
If you want happiness, provide it to others.

Frank Tyger

<u>Journaling Exercise: Write your thoughts below.</u>

Day 160

Happiness is a sunbeam which may pass through a thousand bosoms without losing a particle of its original ray; nay, when it strikes on a kindred heart, like the converged light on a mirror, it reflects itself with redoubled brightness. It is not perfected till it is shared.

Jane Porter

Journaling Exercise: Write your thoughts below.

Day 161

The pursuit of happiness is a most ridiculous phrase: if you pursue happiness you'll never find it.

Carrie P. Snow

Journaling Exercise: Write your thoughts below.

.

Day 162

Each time you step off your path and give someone an act of kindness...then your road to happiness just got a little smoother.

Donna A. Favors

Journaling Exercise: Write your thoughts below.

Day 163

What can be added to the happiness of a man who is in health, out of debt, and has a clear conscience?

Adam Smith

<u>Journaling Exercise: Write your thoughts below.</u>

Day 164
Happiness is a virtue, not its reward.

Baruch Spinoza

Journaling Exercise: Write your thoughts below.

Day 165
Happiness is realizing that nothing is too important.

Antonio Gala

Journaling Exercise: Write your thoughts below.

Day 166

Ever since happiness heard your name, it has been running through the streets trying to find you.

Hafiz of Persia

Journaling Exercise: Write your thoughts below.

Day 167

One can be very happy without demanding that others agree with them.

Ira Gershwin

Journaling Exercise: Write your thoughts below.

Day 168

Even a happy life cannot be without a measure of darkness, and the word happiness would lose its meaning if it were not balanced by sadness.

Alishia Southall

<u>Journaling Exercise: Write your thoughts below.</u>

Day 169

It is the paradox of life that the way to miss pleasure is to seek it first. The very first condition of lasting happiness is that a life should be full of purpose, aiming at something outside self.

Hugo Black

Journaling Exercise: Write your thoughts below.

Day 170

Some days there won't be a song in your heart. Sing anyway.

Emory Austin

<u>Journaling Exercise: Write your thoughts below.</u>

Day 171

If you have not taken the time to define what happiness means to you, what have your spent your whole life pursuing?

Bo Bennett

Journaling Exercise: Write your thoughts below.

Day 172

Different men seek happiness in different ways and by different means.

Aristotle

Journaling Exercise: Write your thoughts below.

Day 173
Happiness is activity.

Aristotle

<u>Journaling Exercise: Write your thoughts below.</u>

Day 174
Happiness never lays its finger on its pulse.

Adam Smith

<u>Journaling Exercise: Write your thoughts below.</u>

Day 175

I am happy and content because I think I am

                                        Alain Rene Lesage

<u>Journaling Exercise: Write your thoughts below.</u>

Day 176

Happiness is largely a matter of self-hypnotism. You can think yourself happy or you can think yourself miserable.

Dorothy Dix

Journaling Exercise: Write your thoughts below.

Day 177

He who loves 50 people has 50 woes; he who loves no one has no woes.

Buddha

<u>Journaling Exercise: Write your thoughts below.</u>

Day 178

Happiness cannot come from without. It must come from within. It is not what we see and touch or that which others do for us which makes us happy; it is that which we think and feel and do, first for the other fellow and then for ourselves.

Helen Keller

Journaling Exercise: Write your thoughts below.

Day 179

No true and permanent fame can be founded except in labors which promote the happiness of mankind

Charles Sumner

Journaling Exercise: Write your thoughts below.

Day 180

By heaven we understand a state of happiness infinite in degree, and endless in duration.

Benjamin Franklin

Journaling Exercise: Write your thoughts below.

Day 181

Many people think that if they were only in some other place, or had some other job, they would be happy. Well, that is doubtful. So get as much happiness out of what you are doing as you can and don't put off being happy until some future date.

Dale Carnegie

Journaling Exercise: Write your thoughts below.

Day 182

Happy trails to you, until we meet again.

Dale Evans Rogers

Journaling Exercise: Write your thoughts below.

Day 183

Happiness is composed of misfortunes avoided.

Alphonse Karr

Journaling Exercise: Write your thoughts below.

Day 184

May God grant you always...A sunbeam to warm you, a moonbeam to charm you, a sheltering Angel so nothing can harm you. Laughter to cheer you. Faithful friends near you. And whenever you pray, Heaven to hear you.

An Irish Blessing

Journaling Exercise: Write your thoughts below.

Day 185

"I'll be happy when...." is the way many people think they are living their lives. Yet, happiness is not something that happens to you. Happiness is inside you now. You are motivated from within. You only have to allow happiness to surface.

John G Agno

Journaling Exercise: Write your thoughts below.

Day 186

Happiness can be found, even in the darkest of times, if one only remembers to turn on the light.

Albus Dumbledore

Journaling Exercise: Write your thoughts below.

Day 187

There comes a time in life, when you walk away from all the drama and the people who create it. You surround yourself with people who make you laugh, forget the bad, and focus on the good. So, love the people who treat you right. Forget about the ones who don't. Life is too short to be anything but happy. Falling down is part of LIFE ...... Getting back up is LIVING.

Female Imagination website

Journaling Exercise: Write your thoughts below.

Day 188

When I was 5 years old, my mother always told me that happiness was the key to life. When I went to school, they asked me what I wanted to be when I grew up. I wrote down 'happy'. They told me I didn't understand the assignment, and I told them they didn't understand life.

John Lennon

Journaling Exercise: Write your thoughts below.

Day 189
I'd rather lose myself in passion than lose my passion.

Jacques Mayol

<u>Journaling Exercise: Write your thoughts below.</u>

Day 190

Happiness is where we find it, but rarely where we seek it.

Anonymous

Journaling Exercise: Write your thoughts below.

Day 191

No matter how dull, or how mean, or how wise a man is, he feels that happiness is his indisputable right.

Helen Keller

Journaling Exercise: Write your thoughts below.

Day 192

Happiness lies not in the mere possession of money; it lies in the enjoyment of achievement, in the thrill of creative effort.

Franklin D. Roosevelt

Journaling Exercise: Write your thoughts below.

Day 193

Happiness in the ordinary sense is not what one needs in life, though one is right to aim at it. The true satisfaction is to come through, and see those whom one lives come through.

E. M. Forster

Journaling Exercise: Write your thoughts below.

Day 194

It is not in the pursuit of happiness that we find fulfillment, it is in the happiness of pursuit.

Denis Waitley

Journaling Exercise: Write your thoughts below.

Day 195

To find recreation in amusement is not happiness.

Blaise Pascal

Journaling Exercise: Write your thoughts below.

Day 196

We are never happy; we can only remember that we were so once.

Alexander Smith

Journaling Exercise: Write your thoughts below.

Day 197
To buy happiness is to sell one's soul.

Doug Horton

<u>Journaling Exercise: Write your thoughts below.</u>

Day 198
Happiness is the harvest of a quiet eye.

Austin O'Malley

Journaling Exercise: Write your thoughts below.

Day 199

It is the conscious man or woman who finds the secret of happiness and contentment; and that, surely, is the ultimate success.

Barry Long

<u>Journaling Exercise: Write your thoughts below.</u>

Day 200

It's never too late—never too late to start over, never too late to be happy.

Jane Fonda

<u>Journaling Exercise: Write your thoughts below.</u>

Day 201

Everything has its wonders, even darkness and silence, and I learn, whatever state I may be in, therein to be content.

Helen Keller

<u>Journaling Exercise: Write your thoughts below.</u>

Day 202

Happiness isn't gained by achieving, it's gained by believing.

Charles Robert Simmons II

Journaling Exercise: Write your thoughts below.

Day 203

The ideals which have always shone before me and filled me with the joy of living are goodness, beauty, and truth. To make a goal of comfort or happiness has never appealed to me; a system of ethics built on this basis would be sufficient only for a herd of cattle.

Albert Einstein

Journaling Exercise: Write your thoughts below.

Day 204

Happiest are the people who give most happiness to others.

Denis Diderot

Journaling Exercise: Write your thoughts below.

Day 205

While we are focusing on fear, worry, or hate, it is not possible for us to be experiencing happiness, enthusiasm or love.

Bo Bennett

Journaling Exercise: Write your thoughts below.

Day 206

Reader, I wish thee Health, Wealth, Happiness, And may kind Heaven thy Year's Industry bless.

Benjamin Franklin

Journaling Exercise: Write your thoughts below.

Day 207

I am happy whatever you become; just remain truthful and sincere to your own being.

Bhagwan Shree Rajneesh

<u>Journaling Exercise: Write your thoughts below.</u>

Day 208

The non-permanent appearance of happiness and distress, and their disappearance in due course, are like the appearance and disappearance of summer and winter seasons.

Bhagavad Gita

Journaling Exercise: Write your thoughts below.

Day 209

As Aristotle said, happiness is not a condition that is produced or stands on its own; rather, it is a frame of mind that accompanies an activity. But another frame of mind comes first. It is a steely determination to do well.

George F. Will

Journaling Exercise: Write your thoughts below.

Day 210

You can pursue happiness by wearing a torn jersey. You can catch it by being good at something you love.

George F. Will

Journaling Exercise: Write your thoughts below.

Day 211

If someday they say of me that in my work I have contributed something to the welfare and happiness of my fellow man, I shall be satisfied.

George Westinghouse

Journaling Exercise: Write your thoughts below.

Day 212

Life at its noblest leaves mere happiness far behind; and indeed cannot endure it. Happiness is not the object of life: life has no object. It is an end in itself; and courage consists in the readiness to sacrifice happiness for a more intense quality.

George Bernard Shaw

Journaling Exercise: Write your thoughts below.

Day 213

Now that I am ninety-five years old, looking back over the years, I have seen many changes taking place, so many inventions have been made. Things now go faster. In olden times things were not so rushed. I think people were more content, more satisfied with life than they are today. You don't hear nearly as much laughter and shouting as you did in my day, and what was fun for us wouldn't be fun now.... In this age I don't think people are as happy, they are worried. They're too anxious to get ahead of their neighbors, they are striving and striving to get something better. I do think in a way that they have too much now. We did with much less.

Grandma Moses

Journaling Exercise: Write your thoughts below.

Day 214

Perfect harmony of body and mind are my key to personal balance and happiness.

Gabriela Sabatini

Journaling Exercise: Write your thoughts below.

Day 215
Happiness... consists in giving, and in serving others.

Henry Drummond

<u>Journaling Exercise: Write your thoughts below.</u>

Day 216

To attain happiness in another world we need only to believe something, while to secure it in this world we must do something.

Charlotte Perkins Gilman

Journaling Exercise: Write your thoughts below.

Day 217

[Wisdom is] the science of happiness or of the means of attaining the lasting contentment which consists in the continual achievement of a greater perfection or at least in variations of the same degree of perfection.

G. Wilhelm Leibniz

Journaling Exercise: Write your thoughts below.

Day 218

The Grand essentials of happiness are: something to do, something to love, and something to hope for.

Allan K. Chalmers

<u>Journaling Exercise: Write your thoughts below.</u>

Day 219

You can't get to happily ever after without turning the page.

Doug Kirchhofer

Journaling Exercise: Write your thoughts below.

Day 220

Goals are a means to an end, not the ultimate purpose of our lives. They are simply a tool to concentrate our focus and move us in a direction. The only reason we really pursue goals is to cause ourselves to expand and grow. Achieving goals by themselves will never make us happy in the long term; it's who you become, as you overcome the obstacles necessary to achieve your goals, that can give you the deepest and most long-lasting sense of fulfillment.

Anthony Robbins

Journaling Exercise: Write your thoughts below.

Day 221

Those who bring sunshine into the lives of others, cannot keep it from themselves.

James Matthew Barrie

Journaling Exercise: Write your thoughts below.

Day 222

Seek to do good, and you will find that happiness will run after you.

James Freeman Clarke

Journaling Exercise: Write your thoughts below.

Day 223

When you realize how perfect everything is you will tilt your head back and laugh at the sky.

Buddha

Journaling Exercise: Write your thoughts below.

Day 224

May you never forget what is worth remembering, nor ever remember what is best forgotten.

An Irish Blessing

Journaling Exercise: Write your thoughts below.

Day 225

There are two ways of spreading light: to be the candle or the mirror that reflects it.

Edith Wharton

Journaling Exercise: Write your thoughts below.

Day 226

Bring love and peace and happiness and beautiful lives into the world in my honor. Thank you. Love you.

Aron Ralston

Journaling Exercise: Write your thoughts below.

Day 227
A happy life consists in tranquillity of mind.

                                            Cicero

Journaling Exercise: Write your thoughts below.

Day 228

I really think happiness is very closely aligned with success, and may almost be an interchangeable synonym. Happiness (like success) also comes from doing what we feel called to do in life; however, it's also obvious no one can experience one without the other.

Donna Fargo

Journaling Exercise: Write your thoughts below.

Day 229

Happiness is a thing to be practiced, like the violin.

John Lubbock

<u>Journaling Exercise: Write your thoughts below.</u>

Day 230

There's a lot to be happy about right now.

Cameron Clapp

<u>Journaling Exercise: Write your thoughts below.</u>

Day 231

Happiness in the present is only shattered by comparison with the past.

Doug Horton

Day 232

When we show concern for the happiness in others, we ultimately enhance the happiness in ourselves.

Donna A. Favors

Journaling Exercise: Write your thoughts below.

Day 233
We are never happy until we learn to laugh at ourselves.

Dorothy Dix

<u>Journaling Exercise: Write your thoughts below.</u>

Day 234

If you're happy in what you're doing, you'll like yourself, you'll have inner peace. And if you have that, along with physical health, you will have had more success than you could possibly have imagined.

Johnny Carson

Journaling Exercise: Write your thoughts below.

Day 235

We learn the inner secret of happiness when we learn to direct our inner drives, our interest and our attention to something besides ourselves.

Ethel Percy Andrus

Journaling Exercise: Write your thoughts below.

Day 236

There is no 'Key to Happiness'...the door is always open.

Anonymous

Journaling Exercise: Write your thoughts below.

Day 237

Don't waste a minute not being happy. If one window closes, run to the next window- or break down a door.

Brooke Shields

Journaling Exercise: Write your thoughts below.

Day 238

The best of all gifts around any Christmas tree: the presence of a happy family all wrapped up in each other.

Burton Hillis

Journaling Exercise: Write your thoughts below.

Day 239

People rarely succeed unless they have fun in what they are doing.

Dale Carnegie

Journaling Exercise: Write your thoughts below.

Day 240

If you want to be happy for a year, plant a garden; If you want to be happy for life, plant a tree.

English Proverb

Journaling Exercise: Write your thoughts below.

Day 241

Life is an Amazing, Hard, Wonderful and Terrible Thing and we never come out of it alive... so live it!

Female Imagination

<u>Journaling Exercise: Write your thoughts below.</u>

Day 242

The common denominator of happy and successful people is that they spend their time with other happy and successful people.

Jeffrey Benjamin

Journaling Exercise: Write your thoughts below.

Day 243

Play with life, laugh with life, dance lightly with life, and smile at the riddles of life, knowing that life's only true lessons are writ small in the margin.

Jonathan Lockwood Huie

Journaling Exercise: Write your thoughts below.

Day 244

Joy blooms where minds and hearts are open.

Jonathan Lockwood Huie

Journaling Exercise: Write your thoughts below.

Day 245

Give a man health and a course to steer, and he'll never stop to trouble about whether he's happy or not.

George Bernard Shaw

Journaling Exercise: Write your thoughts below.

Day 246

Your destiny is my destiny. Your happiness is my happiness.

Islom Karimov

Journaling Exercise: Write your thoughts below.

Day 247

It's a kind of spiritual snobbery that makes people think they can be happy without money.

Albert Camus

Journaling Exercise: Write your thoughts below.

Day 248
Everybody is happy in Switzerland.

Jakob Kolliker

Journaling Exercise: Write your thoughts below.

Day 249

When you realize how much there is to be thankful for and then express that thanks, joy is your natural companion.

Female Imagination website

Journaling Exercise: Write your thoughts below.

Day 250

The full measure of our personal happiness is dictated by how much we offer of ourselves in helping others.

G. Brian Benson

Journaling Exercise: Write your thoughts below.

Day 251

Since you get more joy out of giving joy to others, you should put a good deal of thought into the happiness that you are able to give.

Eleanor Roosevelt

Journaling Exercise: Write your thoughts below.

Day 252

When you look around, what do you see? If you have faith, everything is a miracle and every one is a blessing. If you have none, no thing and no one can make you happy...

John B. Bejo

Journaling Exercise: Write your thoughts below.

Day 253

Simplicity, simplicity, simplicity! We are happy in proportion to the things we can do without.

Henry David Thoreau

Journaling Exercise: Write your thoughts below.

Day 254

Between the tears of sadness and the tears of happiness, there falls the tears of emptiness.

Aidan Naj

Journaling Exercise: Write your thoughts below.

Day 255

The possibility of stepping into a higher plane is quite real for everyone. It requires no force or effort or sacrifice. It involves little more than changing our ideas about what is normal.

Deepak Chopra

Journaling Exercise: Write your thoughts below.

Day 256

Happiness is really an attitude, a state of mind. You can be happy amidst chaos & turmoil, or be miserable amidst order & peace.

Cale Chew

Journaling Exercise: Write your thoughts below.

Day 257

Health is the first benefit. Content is the fortune. Friendliness is the first kindness. Nirvana is the first happiness.

Buddha

Journaling Exercise: Write your thoughts below.

Day 258

May the saddest day of your future be no worse than the happiest day of your past.

Irish Blessings

Journaling Exercise: Write your thoughts below.

Day 259

The law of a good start: Start your morning with a smile. You don't need any reason to smile. Just smile to yourself first. If you can't smile, force yourself to smile anytime of the day. It boosts your immune system and radiates happiness around you.

John B. Bejo

Journaling Exercise: Write your thoughts below.

Day 260

Life begins with attitude. That's why we're called human beings; not human doings.

Dan Waldschmidt

Journaling Exercise: Write your thoughts below.

Day 261

Nothing is permanent. That means life is not done with you yet. Keep changing. Keep evolving. Keep getting better. Explore. Risk. Love. Be happy...

John B. Bejo

<u>Journaling Exercise: Write your thoughts below.</u>

Day 262

Follow your heart. Avoid the crowd. Believe your dreams are worth all the effort.

Dan Waldschmidt

Journaling Exercise: Write your thoughts below.

Day 263
Happiness is a state of mind that only can be gifted by you.

Jeffrey Benjamin

<u>Journaling Exercise: Write your thoughts below.</u>

Day 264

The secret of being miserable is to have the leisure to bother about whether you are happy or not. The cure is occupation.

George Bernard Shaw

Journaling Exercise: Write your thoughts below.

Day 265

The type of Buddhist practices that I talk about in 'The Art of Happiness' have to do with reconditioning one's way of thinking and one's outlook, and one's perception and how one relates to people, ... That type of thing, any Westerner can practice at any time.

Howard Cutler

<u>Journaling Exercise: Write your thoughts below.</u>

Day 266

Happiness comes when we test our skills towards some meaningful purpose.

John Stossel

Journaling Exercise: Write your thoughts below.

Day 267

The road to happiness lies in two simple principles: find what it is that interests you and that you can do well and when you find it, put your whole soul into it....every bit of energy, ambition and natural ability you have.

John D. Rockefeller III

Journaling Exercise: Write your thoughts below.

Day 268

The whole art of teaching is the only art of awakening the natural curiosity of young minds for the purpose of satisfying it afterwards; and curiosity itself can be vivid and wholesome only in proportion as the mind is contented and happy.

Anatole France

Journaling Exercise: Write your thoughts below.

Day 269

Happiness held is the seed; Happiness shared is the flower-Author Unknown People need your love the most when they appear to deserve it the least.

John Harrigan

Journaling Exercise: Write your thoughts below.

Day 270

In our daily lives, we must see that it is not happiness that makes us grateful, but the gratefulness that makes us happy.

Albert Clarke

Journaling Exercise: Write your thoughts below.

Day 271

Happiness consists in activity—it is a running stream, not a stagnant pool.

John Mason

Journaling Exercise: Write your thoughts below.

Day 272

A person will be just about as happy as they make up their minds to be.

Abraham Lincoln

Journaling Exercise: Write your thoughts below.

Day 273

Sorrow comes to all...Perfect relief is not possible, except with time. You cannot now realize that you will ever feel better and yet you are sure to be happy again.

Abraham Lincoln

Journaling Exercise: Write your thoughts below.

Day 274

How strange is the lot of us mortals! Each of us is here for a brief sojourn; for what purpose we know not, though sometimes sense it. But we know from daily life that we exist for other people first of all for whose smiles and well-being our own happiness depends.

Albert Einstein

Journaling Exercise: Write your thoughts below.

Day 275

Happiness is not having what you want, but wanting what you have.

H. Schachtel

Journaling Exercise: Write your thoughts below.

Day 276

You traverse the world in search of happiness, which is within the reach of every man. A contented mind confers it on all.

Horace

Journaling Exercise: Write your thoughts below.

Day 277

He who desires happiness must strive after a perfectly contented disposition and control himself, for happiness has contentment for its root, the root of unhappiness is the contrary disposition.

Guru Nanak

Journaling Exercise: Write your thoughts below.

Day 278

Peace and happiness shall fill your mind deep within, if you act according to truth and self-discipline.

Guru Gobind Singh

Journaling Exercise: Write your thoughts below.

Day 279

Curiosity is one of the great secrets of happiness.

Bryant H. McGill

Journaling Exercise: Write your thoughts below.

Day 280
There's going to be the happy and unhappy.

Betty Gray

Journaling Exercise: Write your thoughts below.

Day 281

The one, who is benevolent and liberal enjoys peace, happiness and prosperity.

Atharva Veda

Journaling Exercise: Write your thoughts below.

Day 282

I also knew that, although infinitely slower, the only real path to personal health and happiness was through my own slow and painful understanding.

Dirk Benedict

Journaling Exercise: Write your thoughts below.

Day 283

Success is getting and achieving what you want. Happiness is wanting and being content with what you get.

Bernard Meltzer

Journaling Exercise: Write your thoughts below.

Day 284

These wise people, meditative, steady, always possessed of strong powers, attain to immortality, the highest happiness.

Friedrich Max Muller

Journaling Exercise: Write your thoughts below.

Day 285

Happiness is being on the beam with life - to feel the pull of life.

Agnes Martin

<u>Journaling Exercise: Write your thoughts below.</u>

Day 286

Joy in looking and comprehending is nature's most beautiful gift.

Albert Einstein

Journaling Exercise: Write your thoughts below.

Day 287

Let the wise guard their thoughts, which are difficult to perceive, extremely subtle, and wander at will. Thought which is well guarded is the bearer of happiness.

Buddha

Journaling Exercise: Write your thoughts below.

Day 288

The happy life is thought to be one of excellence; now an excellent life requires exertion, and does not consist in amusement.

Aristotle

Journaling Exercise: Write your thoughts below.

Day 289

Happiness is the highest good, being a realization and perfect practice of virtue, which some can attain, while others have little or none of it.

Aristotle

Journaling Exercise: Write your thoughts below.

Day 290

Peace of mind is the highest human good and it is your normal, natural condition. Ask yourself, do you want to be right, or do you want to be happy?

Brian Tracy

Journaling Exercise: Write your thoughts below.

Day 291

Forget about likes and dislikes. They are of no consequence. Just do what must be done. This may not be happiness but it is greatness.

George Bernard Shaw

Journaling Exercise: Write your thoughts below.

Day 292

If you conduct yourself as though you expect to be successful and happy, you will seldom be disappointed.

Brian Tracy

Journaling Exercise: Write your thoughts below.

Day 293

At the end of our time on earth, if we have lived fully, we will not be able to say, 'I was always happy.' Hopefully, we will be able to say, 'I have experienced a lifetime of real moments, and many of them were happy moments.'

Barbara Deangelis

Journaling Exercise: Write your thoughts below.

Day 294

When we recall Christmas past, we usually find that the simplest things - not the great occasions - give off the greatest glow of happiness.

Bob Hope

Journaling Exercise: Write your thoughts below.

Day 295

Beauty and happiness and life are all the same and they are pervasive, unattached and abstract and they are our only concern. They are immeasurable, completely lacking in substance. They are perfect and sublime. This is the subject matter of art.

Agnes Martin

Journaling Exercise: Write your thoughts below.

Day 296

Happiness is a sort of atmosphere you can live in sometimes when you're lucky.

Adela Rogers St. Johns

Journaling Exercise: Write your thoughts below.

Day 297

No one can be great, or good, or happy except through the inward efforts of themselves.

Frederick W. Robertson

<u>Journaling Exercise: Write your thoughts below.</u>

Day 298

You know the Stone, was not really such a wonderful thing. As much money and life as you could want! The two things most human beings would choose above all—the trouble is, humans do have a knack for choosing precisely those things that are worst for them.

Albus Dumbledore to Harry Potter, by J.K. Rowling

Journaling Exercise: Write your thoughts below.

Day 299

Love like you've never been hurt because every 60 seconds you spend angry or upset is a minute of happiness you'll never get back...

Unknown

Journaling Exercise: Write your thoughts below.

Day 300
No one is happy all his life long.

Euripides

Journaling Exercise: Write your thoughts below.

Day 301

Joy is not the result of getting what you want; it is the way to get what you want. In the deepest sense, joy is what you want.

Alan Cohen

Journaling Exercise: Write your thoughts below.

Day 302

A search for true happiness is found when you look no further than your forehead.

Jeffrey Benjamin

Journaling Exercise: Write your thoughts below.

Day 303

A smile can cause a chain reaction of happiness.

Eduardo Monroy

<u>Journaling Exercise: Write your thoughts below.</u>

Day 304

Those painful memories are what can help us make it to tomorrow, and become stronger. That goes for everyone. Every single human being has that power within them. Walk tall. And I, too, will forever walk tall, ever onwards. Never forget the memories we share.

Augie

Journaling Exercise: Write your thoughts below.

Day 305

People spend a lifetime searching for happiness. Looking for peace. They chase idle dreams, religions, even other people, hoping to fill the emptiness that plagues them. The irony is the only place they ever needed to search was within.

Female Imagination website

Journaling Exercise: Write your thoughts below.

Day 306

Only a man who has felt ultimate despair is capable of feeling ultimate bliss.

Alexandre Dumas Pere

Journaling Exercise: Write your thoughts below.

Day 307

In order to be utterly happy the only thing necessary is to refrain from comparing this moment with other moments in the past, which I often did not fully enjoy because I was comparing them with other moments of the future.

Andre Gide

Journaling Exercise: Write your thoughts below.

Day 308

Be happy. Be you.

Jenni Fitzpatrick

<u>Journaling Exercise: Write your thoughts below.</u>

Day 309

We're constantly striving for success, fame and comfort when all we really need to be happy is someone or some thing to be enthusiastic about.

H. Jackson Brown Jr.

Journaling Exercise: Write your thoughts below.

Day 310

A journey shared brings more happiness than one completed alone.

Jeff Lowe

Journaling Exercise: Write your thoughts below.

Day 311

Happiness begins with love from others, but ends if you can't love yourself.

Jeffrey Benjamin

Journaling Exercise: Write your thoughts below.

Day 312

In order for the light to illuminate the darkness must first be there. Same way how success needs failure and happiness needs sorrow.

Armando Rodriguez Jr.

Journaling Exercise: Write your thoughts below.

Day 313
Happiness is the language of the soul.

Ashish Sophat

Journaling Exercise: Write your thoughts below.

Day 314

TRUE happiness is a state of fulfillment.

Ashish Sophat

<u>Journaling Exercise: Write your thoughts below.</u>

Day 315
Smile in all that you do, it might just make someone's day!

Jeffrey Coleman Jr.

<u>Journaling Exercise: Write your thoughts below.</u>

Day 316

Optimism may not always deliver the results I want, but I'll take my chances at it.

Anya Sundquist

Journaling Exercise: Write your thoughts below.

Day 317

The beauty of life does not depend on how happy you are... but on how happy others can because of you!!!

Author unknown

Journaling Exercise: Write your thoughts below.

Day 318
Joy lives concealed in grief.

Jalal ad-Din Rumi

Journaling Exercise: Write your thoughts below.

Day 319
Recipe for a happy heart:
2 cups of Love,
1 cup of Friendship,
1 cup of Gratitude,
...Add a dash of Laughter,
... Pour into a Soul.

Female Imagination website

Journaling Exercise: Write your thoughts below.

Day 320

Without forgiveness, you cannot move forward on your journey through life and happiness.

B A Lingle

Journaling Exercise: Write your thoughts below.

Day 321

Simplify your life, faith, home, expectations of self & others. Walk in God's love & light. Become more aware. Live NOW, it's the only sure thing. The next moment, a possible gift.

Angel Dykes

Journaling Exercise: Write your thoughts below.

Day 322

A grain of sand, a drop of water, a view for endless miles, no person can comprehend, were just a speck in the sea of life. Live every day, live every moment, embrace live , enjoy life, be Happy!!!

Franco C. Zarli Jr.

Journaling Exercise: Write your thoughts below.

Day 323
To get happy you have to give happy.

Chris Brady

Journaling Exercise: Write your thoughts below.

Day 324

If you want to be happy value and cherish every little thing in life, even the small things. Everything and every second in life is valuable and precious to our own existence, happiness and self-worth.

Brandon Hofer

Journaling Exercise: Write your thoughts below.

Day 325

The summit of happiness is reached when a person is ready to be what he is.

Desiderius

Journaling Exercise: Write your thoughts below.

Day 326

A huge part of happiness is to understand that good things fall apart so better things can fall together.

Jenna Dawn Frasure

Journaling Exercise: Write your thoughts below.

Day 327

Happiness is not a brilliant climax to years of grim struggle and anxiety. It is a long succession of little decisions simply to be happy in the moment.

J. Donald Walters

<u>Journaling Exercise: Write your thoughts below.</u>

Day 328

Look to yourself to find happiness. No one is so powerful to do it for you, or to take it away from you.

George Zaharis

Journaling Exercise: Write your thoughts below.

Day 329

There are two main emotions that humans possess, fear & love. Fear keeps you from finding joy, happiness, laughter and love. Love brings about joy, happiness and laughter. Keep looking for the love in everything around you and you will succeed in filling the well of life and sharing it with others.

Celestine L. Gray

<u>Journaling Exercise: Write your thoughts below.</u>

Day 330

True happiness is not about a big laugh or tears of joy, it's about a simple smile whenever you remember someone who made your life simple but completely happy.

Jeff Ervin Ramon

Journaling Exercise: Write your thoughts below.

Day 331

Enjoy life and smile. No one can take that away from you unless you allow them to.

Dorian Thomas Von Klaus

Journaling Exercise: Write your thoughts below.

Day 332
Smile when confronted, no one blames the happy person.

                                        Dorian Thomas Von Klaus

<u>Journaling Exercise: Write your thoughts below.</u>

Day 333

Happy are those that listen and obey to the instructions of old.

Gotlieb Nakuumba

Journaling Exercise: Write your thoughts below.

Day 334

Happy are those who find peace, for with peace, all can be happy.

Emanouhl

Journaling Exercise: Write your thoughts below.

Day 335

The way to happiness is finding what you ALREADY have and be GRATEFUL for them.

John B. Bejo

Journaling Exercise: Write your thoughts below.

Day 336

Life is a book with no preface, neither it has a last cover page. We write the book, we set the pace. Not all the stories are written on single page. Sometimes we don't find enough space to reflect on our own grace. Throw away old stress, fall asleep with a smile on ur graceful face.

Abhishek Singh

Journaling Exercise: Write your thoughts below.

Day 337

I have found that I am happiest when I am being creative...
letting source/my gifts/whatever you want to call it come through.
It is one of the few times when I know I am doing exactly what it is
I am supposed to be doing and I can get out of my head and just be
at total peace.

G. Brian Benson

Journaling Exercise: Write your thoughts below.

Day 338

For happiness is not what makes us grateful. It is gratefulness that makes us happy.

David Steindl-Rast

Journaling Exercise: Write your thoughts below.

Day 339

Happiness: If you know what will give you the true and happy life, then you must keep trying until the day you are dying to achieve your happiness.

Abdul Salam

Journaling Exercise: Write your thoughts below.

Day 340

Be happy, be thankful, be YOU. It may seem hard to do, you know, to be happy, and be who you are, but, at least you tried. No regrets. Your happiness is priceless, so don't ever lose it, especially don't lose who you are.

Happy FBI site

Journaling Exercise: Write your thoughts below.

Day 341

You're only down-and-out if you're still lying on the floor. Get up.

Dan Waldschmidt

Journaling Exercise: Write your thoughts below.

Day 342

If life were easier you wouldn't be happier.

Dan Waldschmidt

<u>Journaling Exercise: Write your thoughts below.</u>

Day 343
Never stop moving towards where you want to be.

Dan Waldschmidt

Journaling Exercise: Write your thoughts below.

Day 344

Success and happiness are not about what you are willing to do. They're about what you actually end up doing.

Dan Waldschmidt

Journaling Exercise: Write your thoughts below.

Day 345

This is the true joy of life: the being used up for a purpose recognized by yourself as a mighty one; being a force of nature instead of a feverish, selfish little clot of ailments and grievances, complaining that the world will not devote itself to making you happy.

George Bernard Shaw

Journaling Exercise: Write your thoughts below.

Day 346

Our minds are as different as our faces. We are all traveling to one destination: happiness, but few are going by the same road.

Charles Caleb Colton

Journaling Exercise: Write your thoughts below.

Day 347

Not only is there a right to be happy, there is a duty to be happy. So much sadness exists in the world that we are all under obligation to contribute as much joy as lies within our powers.

John S. Bonnell

Journaling Exercise: Write your thoughts below.

Day 348

Money, or even power, can never yield happiness unless it be accompanied by the goodwill of others.

B.C. Forbes

Journaling Exercise: Write your thoughts below.

Day 349

Did you ever see an unhappy horse? Did you ever see a bird that had the blues? One reason why birds and horses are not unhappy is because they are not trying to impress other birds and horses.

Dale Carnegie

Journaling Exercise: Write your thoughts below.

Day 350

Being Happy is a personal business. That means it's OUR responsibility to make ourselves happy. Don't expect people to give this to you.

John B. Bejo

<u>Journaling Exercise: Write your thoughts below.</u>

Day 351
Simplicity is the essence of happiness.

Cedric Bledsoe

<u>Journaling Exercise: Write your thoughts below.</u>

Day 352

My plea is that we stop seeking out the storms and enjoy more fully the sunlight...I am asking that we look a little deeper for the good, that we still our voices of insult and sarcasm, that we more generously compliment and endorse virtue and effort.

Gordon B. Hinckley

Journaling Exercise: Write your thoughts below.

Day 353

Celebrate kindness. Communicate intention. Concentrate effort.

Dan Waldschmidt

Journaling Exercise: Write your thoughts below.

Day 354

Happiness starts within.

Be real, appreciate what you have, enjoy every moment, spread the love. If everything comes back, consider it as a miracle.

Cherryl Anne Lintag

Journaling Exercise: Write your thoughts below.

Day 355

You can't put your feet in a bucket of water and wonder why you can't seem to catch on fire. Get serious about making a difference. Stop holding back.

Dan Waldschmidt

<u>Journaling Exercise: Write your thoughts below.</u>

Day 356

The road leading from past through present to our future may often look patchy and full of big potholes whose solutions can't be mere repair, resurfacing or refurbishment, but warrant a need to lay a new lane for our happy journey.

Anuj Somany

Journaling Exercise: Write your thoughts below.

Day 357

Dare to try something new. And when you do hit a wall or make a mistake, don't blame anyone else.

Dan Waldschmidt

Journaling Exercise: Write your thoughts below.

Day 358

Lay it all on the line and then cross that line.

Dan Waldschmidt

<u>Journaling Exercise: Write your thoughts below.</u>

Day 359

Without depression and anxiety, I would not be who I am; a person who can see beauty and humour in the smallest and least likely of things; appreciating others kindness tenfold. When the black clouds of despair descend and life seems pointless I try to remember that one day in the future, perhaps this very day, a gentle breeze will blow the clouds away and allow the sunshine in. When that happens the world is a new and magical place and I wish to live forever.

Irene Grodecki

Journaling Exercise: Write your thoughts below.

Day 360

You need to love what you do (in a job) or you need to do what you love.

Fahim Uddin

Journaling Exercise: Write your thoughts below.

Day 361

You draw and design to make a beautiful history, you write and you invent to teach and motivate generations, you sing and dance to be happy, you act to deliver a decent message, you live to give.

Haifa Sanad

Journaling Exercise: Write your thoughts below.

Day 362

Before you can be happy you have to choose to be happy. Once you've made the choice the rest is really rather easy. But before you can choose to be happy you have to first decide that you deserve to be happy. How many of us run head on into this wall of our own construction?

E.R. Rock

Journaling Exercise: Write your thoughts below.

Day 363

The key to true happiness is knowing what will make you happy and how to obtain it.

Andy Stewart

<u>Journaling Exercise: Write your thoughts below.</u>

Day 364

A good smile is less of an outward show of my inward feelings at a certain time, and more of a constant overflow of the love I have in my heart for all of humanity regardless of my own circumstances.

Joey Talladino

Journaling Exercise: Write your thoughts below.

Day 365

Our thoughts are the source of what we begin reaping in our lives. The seeds of thought that we choose to plant can grow into strong sturdy oak trees or into relentlessly spreading poison ivy that infects ourselves and all we touch.

Joey Talladino

Journaling Exercise: Write your thoughts below.

Leap Year - Day 366

The only person that can make you angry, sad or happy is you.

Jeffrey Benjamin

Journaling Exercise: Write your thoughts below.

Bonus Quote 1

Live a life of SIMPLICITY, CONTENTMENT and THANKFULNESS. HAPPINESS and PEACE of MIND will follow with all the days of your lives.

Ebuhaika Ballsteros

Journaling Exercise: Write your thoughts below.

Bonus Quote II

The purpose of human life and the sense of happiness is to give the maximum what the man is able to give.

Alexander Alekhine

<u>Journaling Exercise: Write your thoughts below.</u>

Liked Happiness 365?

Please let us and others know, by leaving a review on the book site that you purchased it.

Get Happiness 365 Quotes direct to your inbox daily.

And be the first to learn of Happiness 365 updates, giveaways, free days and NEW books in the series.

Sign up here:

http://www.kcharry.com/happiness-365-updates/

Connect with Happiness 365 on Social Media

Follow Deena and KC on Twitter:
    Deena: https://twitter.com/DeenaBChopra
    KC: https://twitter.com/kchrissyharry
    And like us on Facebook to join the conversation!
    https://www.facebook.com/pages/Happiness-365/1441747622781692

Made in the USA
Las Vegas, NV
20 April 2022